2

Konami Kanata

contents

homemade 21~38+

homemade 21: a cat is moved

LOOKS LIKE IT'S TIME TO MOVE ON TO DRY FOOD.
I'VE SOAKED IT A BIT.
CAT RAISING
MEOW
TASTY STUFF?
MUNCH MUNCH

SMAK
SMAK
SHOOP

NOT BAD,
I GUESH.

SIP

AHH!

THAT'S GOOD!

PLUNK

IS IT TASTY ?
I'M HAVING SOME!
LAP LAP
PLIP
BLECH
YUCKY!!
...
DASH
SWOOP

YUM!
SIP

CURR

IS THAT TASTY?

CHEW CHEW
CHEW CHEW
CUR

...
CURR

NO THANKS.

IS THAT TASTY?

CHOMP

...

CHI'S IS THE MOST TASTY!

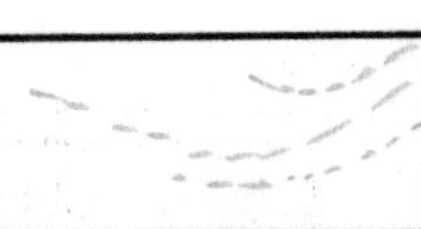

HEY, WHAT A NICE SMELL.

LOOKS YUMMY !!
I PUT LOTS OF BUTTER ON IT.

OPEN WIDE
MEOW
MEOW
IZZIT GOOD? IZZIT TASTY?

TASTY ?!

CHIK

MUNCH MUNCH

IS IT
DELISH
?
RAISE

SHIVER

SO GOOD
!

I CAN'T BELIEVE SUCH A TASTY THING EXISTS.

SMACK
AH
YOINK

GONG
TINK
GRIN

YOHEI
IF CHI WANTS SOME PANCAKE
GIVE HER A LITTLE PIECE.
SSSH

SHIVER

the end

homemade 22: a cat takes a bath
SPLASH SPLASH
WOOHOOO
WHAT'S GOING ON?
FWICH
AND THIS IS WHERE THAT BUBBLY WETNESS HAPPENED.
YAYAAYK
WEIRD

HEY HEY
KLAK
WANNA JOIN US, CHI?
ZING
SKAT

PHEW... THEY SURPRISED ME.
HUFF
COME ON IN, CHI.
YEAH YAY

DO IT AGAIN DAD!
ROGER!
WOO HOO

PUTT PUTT PUTT
KYAA YEAH

WHAT ARE THEY UP TO?

PUTT PUTT PUTT PUTT

YAYAAYK
PUTT
PUTT
PUTT
PUTT
PEEK

I'LL GO CAREFULWY.
SNEAK
SNEAK
SNEAK

IT'S CHI!
SLINK

PUTT
PUTT
PUTT

PUTT
PUTT

KLIK
KLIK
KLIK
MYA
WHAZZAT?

UH...

MYA
EEK!

WET!
MIYA
SO BUSY ...
TINK

LICK
LICK
LICK
LICK

THAT WAS CWOSE.

DAD, CAN WE ADD SOME MORE TOYS?
YAY
OKAY

WOO HOO

KASHA
KASHA

STARE

SPLISH
SPLISH

PLOK PLOK
PLOK
PLOK
HUFF

MYA
SO MANY!
CHI!

SWIP
SWIP
WAIT UP!
MYA MYA !!
YAY!
MIYA
SNATCH
!
I'M FAWLING !!
NO NO NO
FLAP
FLAP
FLAP
PWEASE NO...
SPLASH
WOAH
OH

OH NO!

CHI'S FALLEN IN THE TUB!
GYA!!
SPLASH
SPLASH

ARE YOU OKAY?
GYA!
CHI!
GYA

WELL, CHI LOOKS LIKE SHE'S FINE.
SIGH

BUT SHE MUST HATE BATHING EVEN MORE NOW.

GROAN

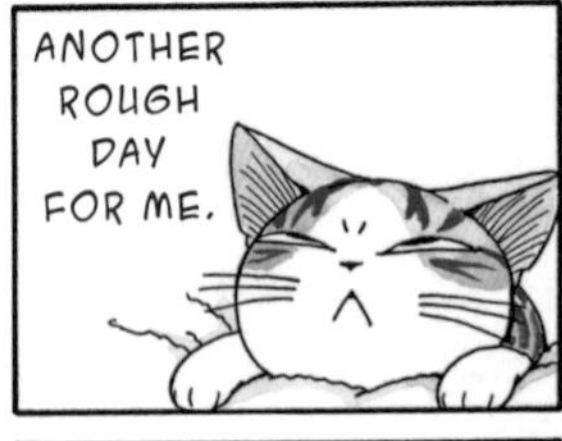
ANOTHER ROUGH DAY FOR ME.

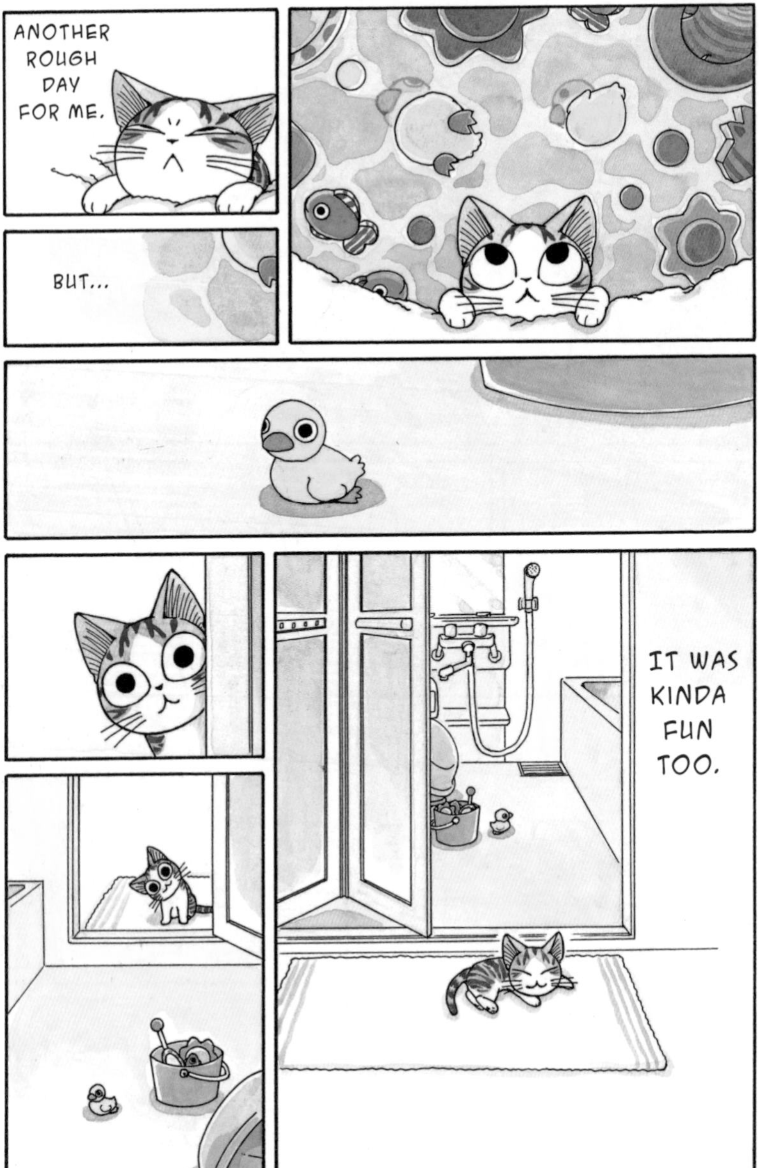

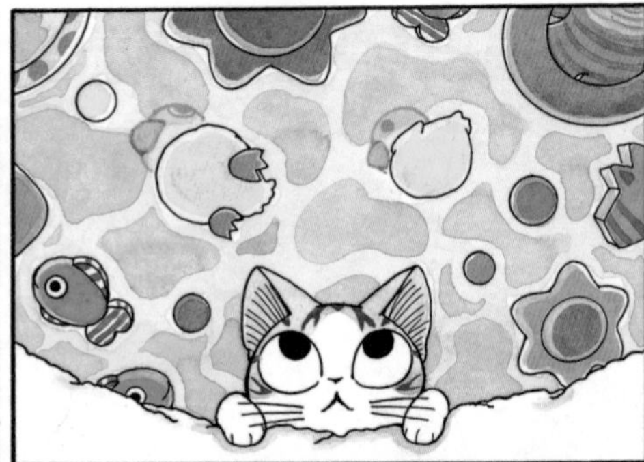

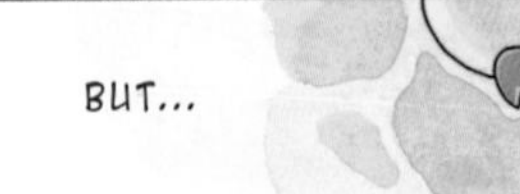
BUT...

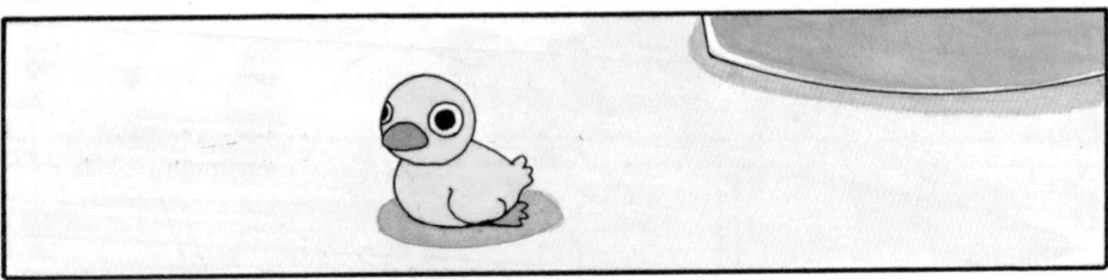

IT WAS KINDA FUN TOO.

the end

homemade 23: a cat throws down

ZZZZ

CHI'S GONNA NAP HERE TOO.

SHFT

FLOP
SWIP
SMAK
SNUGG

ROLL

THUNK
MIGYU

WHAT THE?

...

SHUV
SHUV
SHUV
POP

YOHEY'S
A BAD
SLEEPER.

SNUGGL
SNUGGL

STRETCH
STRETCH
STRETCH

SNUGGL

CHI, YOU'RE A ROUGH SLEEPER.

FLIP

FLOP
ROLL
ROLL
WHUMP
SMUSH
HEY

ENOUGH WITH
THE SMUSHING,
YOHEY.
I'LL
SHLEEP
ALONE.

WAIT...

IT REMINDS ME OF SOME-THING.

BUT WHAT
IZZIT ?

SKOOT
SKOOT

I WONDER.

WEL-
COME
HOME.
IS
YOHEI
ASLEEP
?
YUP.

AW
AND
WITH
CHI.

ZZZ
SNUG

THEY LOOK JUST LIKE

THE DEAREST OF HUMAN SIBLINGS.

HEE HEE

SHOOP

the end

homemade 24: a cat asserts itself

CHI

WHAT A CUTE WAY TO NAP.

EVEWYONE'S HERE

MEOWN
YAY
PRR PRR PRR

I LIKE HER TAIL.
I LIKE HER PAW PADS.
A CAT'S CLAWS ARE PRETTY IMPRESSIVE, TOO.

POKE POKE
RUB RUB RUB
PINCH
PINCH

ARGH...

MEOW!
SO ANNOYING!
ZASH

BLOX

TAP TAP TAP

AH, LOOKS LIKE WE BOTH-ERED HER A BIT.

WIGGL WIGGL

AH, NICE AND QUIET.

A POST-CARD FROM GRAMS ARRIVED TODAY.
OH, RIGHT!
REALLY
READ IT FOR ME!

IT SAYS, "HOW IS MY DEAR YOHEI DOING?"
THEN WHAT?
I'M FINE!

BABBLE
BABBLE
BABBLE

GRAMS IS TAKING A TRIP.
HAH
WOW!
WHERE?
HAH
HAH
TWITCH

WHAT ARE THOSE THREE DOING OVER THERE, HUH?

SAUNTER
SAUNTER
SHOOP
YEAH
HA HA

SAUNTER
SAUNTER

PEEK

YEAH
YEAH
YAH
HEE
HEE

HUB
BUB
KYAA
HA
HA
!

TUMBLE

URGH

OH
YEAH!

CHI'S
OVER
HERE.
PRRR
PRRR
MEW
GLANCE

ROLL
ROLL

CHITTER
CHITTER
CHITTER

HEY?

SKOOT

SKOOT
BOING
BOING
BOING
BOING

PANT
PANT
PANT
PANT

HOW ABOUT THAT?

CHATTER
CACKLE
WOW
...

THAT'S GREAT!
HA HA!
WONDERFUL
SO THEN I...
PLOINK
SHKT SHKT

GLARE

HEY, CHI!
ALWAYS THE CENTER OF ATTENTION.
I CAN'T SEE THE POSTCARD, CHI.
MEOW
STOP IGNOWING ME!

the end

homemade 25: a cat stands firm

SHUK
SHUK

THIS IS MINE!

BURROW

SNATCH

...

GET OUT, CHI!
PLOP

HEY!
MEOWR
THIS IS CHI'S!

GRIP

HMM?
DO I SENSE SOMETHING?
RUSTL

MEOWR
I CRAWLED INTO IT FIRST.

YOINK
ARGH!
!
HEH
KLUTCH
THAT'S CHI'S, LET GO!
MEOW
NO WAY!
I'M USING IT NOW.
RUSTL
THERE IT IS AGAIN.
RUSTL
HOORAY!
YANK
HRM?

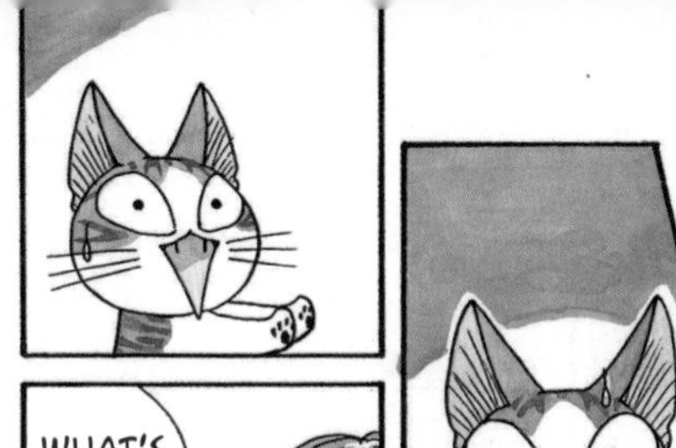

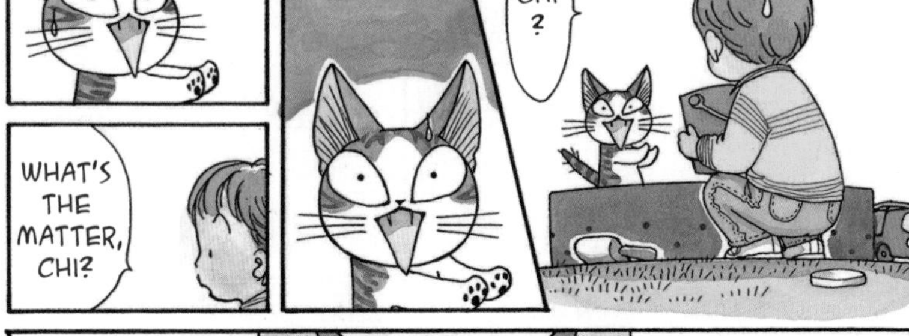
WHAT'S THE MATTER, CHI?
CHI?

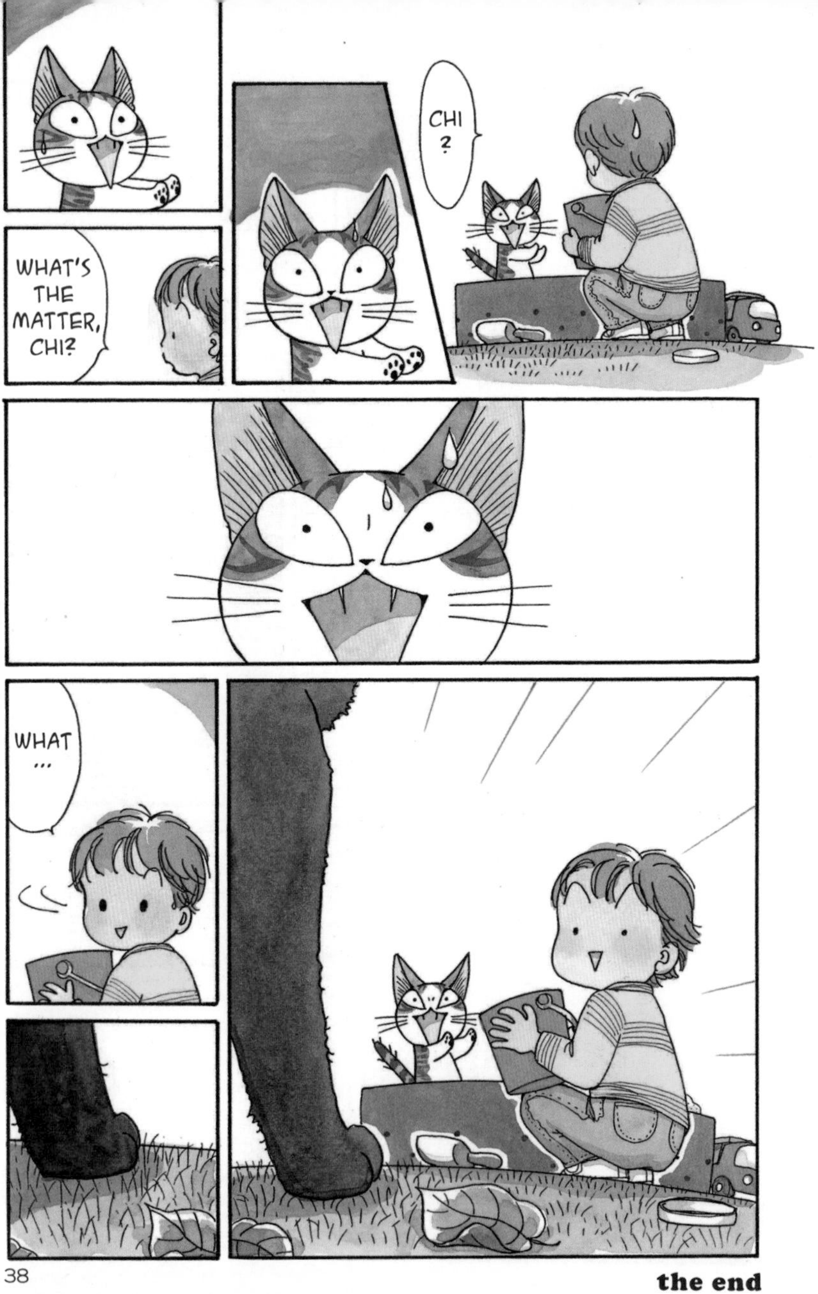

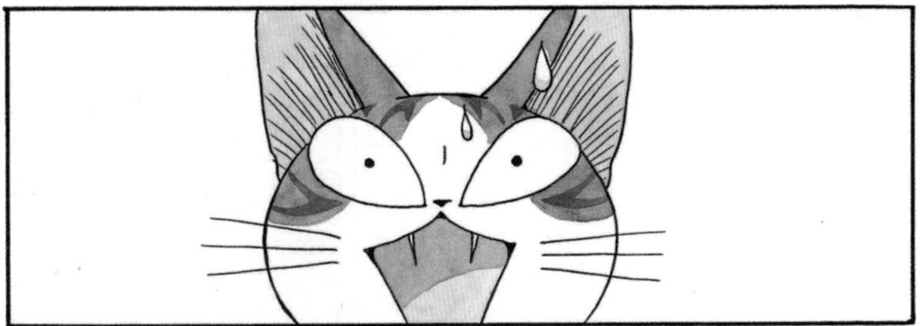

WHAT …

the end

homemade 26: a cat encounters

SNATCH
SKOOT
DART
PLUNK
PHEW!
WHAT A SCARY CAT!
HEY, WHAT WAZZAT?
CREEP
WANDER WANDER WANDER
WOAH!

!
SNIF
SNIF
SNIF
WHAT DO WE DO? IT'S SCARY.
JAUNT JAUNT JAUNT

MEOWRR

GET OUT!
MEOWR

GLARE

RARRR
MEOWR

WHAT NOW? CHI'S IN TROUBLE!

SNIF SNIF
!

HAAAAA

HUP

ZING

SHOO
SHOO

SHOO
GO AWAY!

DAT'S NO GOOD, YOHEY.

SHMP
ZAPT
YOU'RE NOT INVITED!
FSSSK
THIS IS CHI AND CHI'S BUDDIES' HOME
FSSSK
SHOO SHOO!
FSSSK
FOOOM
!!
WHAT'S GO-ING ON?
FMMM

FOOOOM
FOOOE
TAKE THAT!
SHOO!
FSSK

MOVE
SHOO SHOO
FSSK
FWOOE

LUMBER
RUSTL
RUSTL

SHAV

THIS HUGE CAT CAME INTO OUR HOUSE, DAD.
MEOW
IT WAS REALLY CWAZY !
MEOW
MEOW
MEOW
IT EVEN HAD A SCARY FACE, TOO.
LIKE THIS
AND IT WAS HANGING AROUND GLARING AT US.
MEOWR
THE CAT WAS ALL BLACK AND THIS BIG!
IT WAS BIG AND POOFY.
MEW
HMM
I JUST HOPE IT DOESN'T GET WORSE ...
I HEAR IT'S BEEN MAKING APPEARANCES IN OTHER APARTMENTS.
I'M SURE THAT'S THE SAME "BIG CAT" THAT'S BEEN CAUSING A STIR AROUND HERE.

IT'S NOT LIKE WE HAVEN'T GOT CHI HERE.
WHAT A MESS.
AH, CATS ...
HEY, DADDY!
MIU

YOHEY WAS IN REALLY BIG TWOUBLE.
MEOW
CHI WAS IN DANGER, SO I STEPPED IN.

MEW
RIGHT, YOHEY?
BUT...
WHAT WAS THAT STWANGE CWEATURE, ANYWAY?
MYA?

the end

homemade 27: a cat intrudes

UNIVERSE
ART
PAINT
DECORA
ART BOOK
WHATCHA DOING, DADDY?
YOU MIGHT WANT TO LEAVE DAD ALONE TODAY.
WHISPER
DAD'S WORK IS AT A STANDSTILL, SO HE'S IN A FOUL MOOD.

SO TRY TO PLAY AROUND HERE TODAY, OKAY?
UH-HUH

ARGH

TIP
TIP
TIP
TIP
TIP

MEOW!
DADDY, LET'S PLAY!

...

HEY, COME ON!
MEOW
MEOW
UMMM
HRM
HMMM

SHRAK SHRAK
SHOOM

CHUK
THIS WON'T DO.
PLUNK
PLOP
PLOP
RUSTL
RUSTL
WHOA
SKAT
MEOOW
YAAAY!
SKAMPER

ARGH
PLINK

MEW
SO MWUCH FUN!
GNAW GNAW GNAW GNAW

SQWEEK

MIU
ISN'T THIS GREAT, DADDY?

SIGH
CATS HAVE IT EASY.
BATH-ROOM BREAK
SHUMP SHUMP

?

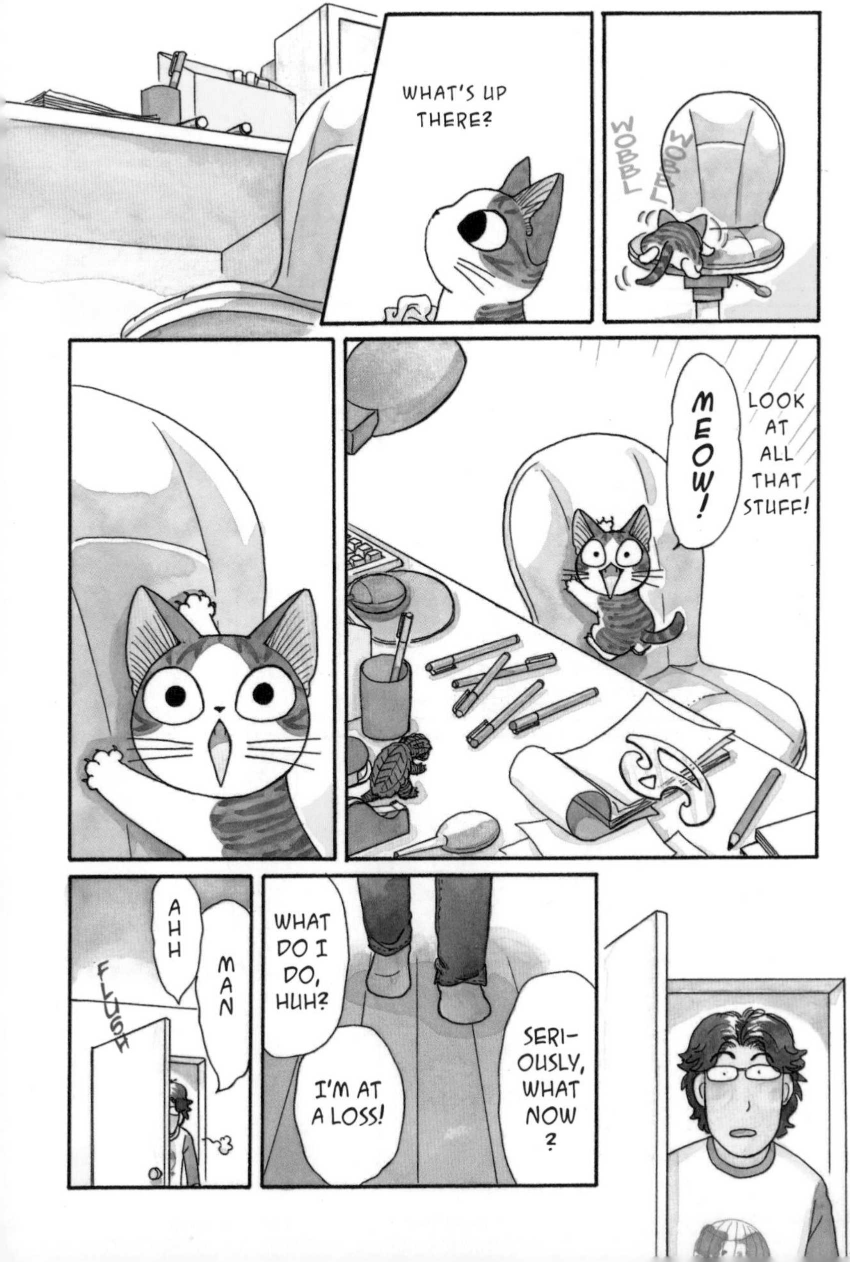

WHAT'S UP THERE?

WOBBL

WOBBL

MEOW!

LOOK AT ALL THAT STUFF!

KLIK KLIK
PHOO
MEOW
THIS IS FUN!
FWAP
FLAP
MEOW
THAT WAS FUNNY.
OH... UM...
UNIVERSE
HUP HUP
HUP
MEOW
WHAT A BWAST!
HUP HUP HUP HUP HUP

MEOWR
WHUMP

WOAH THERE!
BLAM
KRSH
KRSH

STOP, CHI.
AHHH
LOOK AT THAT
WHAT A BIG MESS YOU'VE MADE

OH?

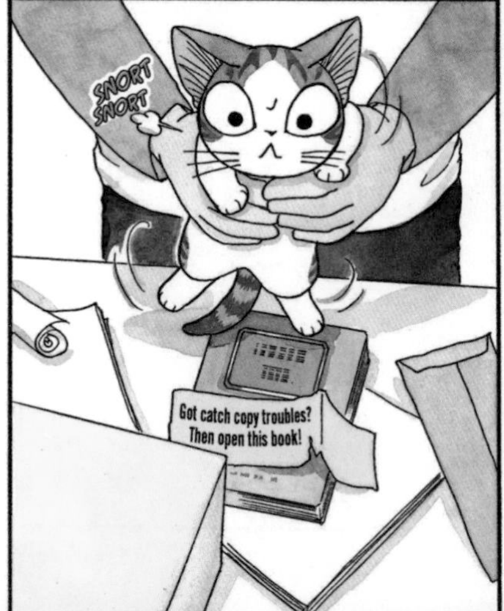
SNORT SNORT
Got catch copy troubles?
Then open this book!

Language
Dictionary
Got catch copy troubles?
Then open this book!

OH!
I'LL USE THIS!
WAY TO GO, CHI!
NUZZL
?
ALL RIGHT! HERE WE GO!

ROOOT-!
MEOW
I WONDER WHAT'S UP WITH DAD?
IS HE PLAYING WITH CHI?
I'M NOT SURE, BUT IT SOUNDS LIKE HE'S HAVING FUN.

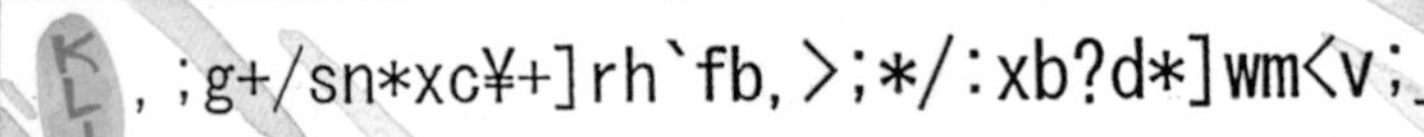

KLIK
, ;g+/sn*xc¥+]rh`fb, >;*/:xb?d*]wm<v;_

KLIK
KLIK
OKAY, LET'S GET BACK TO WORK!
MIYAN
WHAT A BWAST, HUH?
MIYA
DADDY HAS BEEN DOWING FUN STUFF ALL THIS TIME!

the end

homemade 28: a cat is robbed
WHERE'D IT GO?
AND NOW IT BUSTED UP MY FLOWER POTS.
YAMMER YAMMER
ZWASH

!

MIYAN MIYAN
MOMMY, MOMMY, THAT STWANGE THING IS BACK!

THREE WHOLE POTS?!
LOOKS LIKE IT.
AND IT SURE IS FAST.
OH MY!

MOMMY'S NOT HERE.

NEITHER IS DADDY.

NOT EVEN YOHEY.

WELL, YOHEY'D JUST GET IN THE WAY.

VIP

!
IT'S IN THE HOUSE!

IT COULDN'T HAVE GONE FAR.
HOW ABOUT OVER THERE?
CLAMMER CLAMMER

VASH
EEP

...
SO SCAREWY!

BUT

HRMPH
IT'S UP TO ME!

FSSK
GET OUTTA OUR HOME !
SNARL
SNARL
SNARL
!
PAD PAD PAD
PAD
PAD
PAD
PAD
PAD
PAD
PAD
PAD

FWOOM

NO, DON'T STEP ON ME!

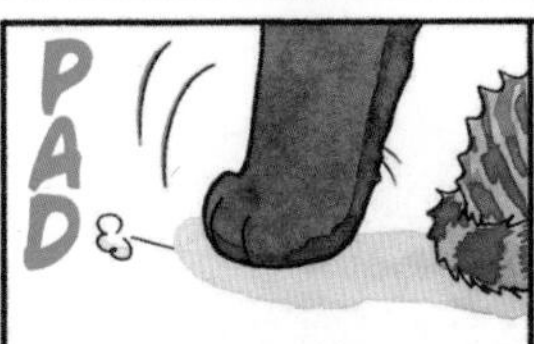
PAD

AH?
PAD
PAD

PAD
PAD
PAD

I WASN'T STOMPED ON.

MUNCH MUNCH

MUNCH MUNCH MUNCH MUNCH
CHOMP CHOMP CHOMP

!
MY FOOD !

HSSS
STOP THAT! IT'S CHI'S FOOD!

SHFT

KRUNCH KRUNCH KRUNCH
KRUNCH
!!

FSSS
DON'T YOU EAT THAT!
BOING
BOING
BOING
KRUNCH
KRUNCH
KRUNCH
KRUNCH
HSSS
STOP IT!
BOING
BOING
KLIP
SPLAT
...
MY FOOD...
PAD
HMM ?

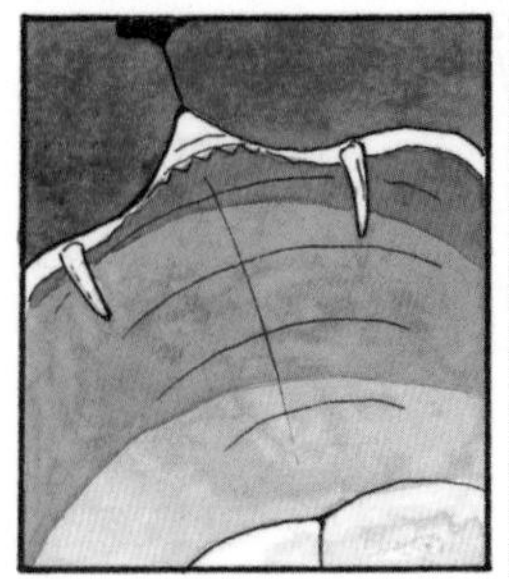

the end

homemade 29: a cat considers
MMMF
...
I'M DONE FOR...
REALLY?!
IT STOLE IT?!

IT HELD IT IN ITS BIG MOUTH.
WOW
IT CHOMPED THE SALMON SLICE AND RAN OFF.

GOOD-NESS.
IT WAS SOME POTS.
LAST WEEK IT WAS MY HOME. TODAY, ON THE 1ST FL,
WHAT A PAIN.

RIGHT
WELL, CATS CAN BE TROU-BLE.

YOINK

PLOP

GAPE

THERE.
NYA

PAD PAD PAD

...

WHAT THE...

FZZZL
SO YOU JUST WANTED TO GET CHI UP?

!
ZAPT

ZING

...

TWINGE
TWINGE
CHI'S SOFT THING !
!

HAAAR!
STOP !
DASH

FWUMP

HAHR!
NO! THIS IS CHI'S!

STARE

GLARE

STARE

MOOSH

WHAT ARE YA DOING?
HSSS

LICK
LICK
LICK

ARE YA GROOMING ME?

NYA
YOUR FUR WAS A MESS.
I GUESH HE'S NOT AS BAD AS HE LOOKS.
BUT, HE DID EAT MY MEAL.
GRR
TURN
ZING
BLAG

LIK LIK
LIK LIK LIK LIK
HOP
NYA
LATER.
SHRK SHRK
PHEW

PLUNK

WHAT A KITTY CRISIS OUT THERE.

ALL GONE.

SHE ATE ALL THAT?

STUFFED HER FACE AND NOW SOUND ASLEEP...
WHAT A LIFE.

I'M SPWENT.

the end

homemade 30: a cat reports

MYA MYA
THAT STWANGER PASSED BY TODAY.
MYA
MEOW
AND IT ENTERED OUR HOME!
CHI'S PRETTY EXCITED TODAY.
SHE HAD QUITE A MEAL, TOO.

WAIT, SHE HAD THAT MUCH?
AND I GAVE HER A HUGE SERVING.
YUP.
SHE ATE ALL HER CAT FOOD.

AND CHI WAS THE ONLY ONE HOME!
MEOW

THAT'S AMAZING, CHI!
REALLY
PAT PAT

MYA
CHI TRIED REALLY HARD.

PAT

DO YA?

GRIN
GRIN
IT SURE MUST HAVE BEEN TASTY.
MEYAR
DO YOU GET IT, DADDY?

I'M HUNGRY!
COME AND GET IT!
PLUNK
MEAL!
MEAL! MY TUMMY'S ALL RUMBLY.
MEOWR
LET'S DIG IN!
HUH?
WHERE'S CHI'S FOOD?
MIYAA

MEAL, MEAL!
MEOW MEOW
MOM, WHAT ABOUT CHI'S FOOD?

NOTHING FOR CHI TONIGHT.
WE CAN'T HAVE HER GET A TUMMY ACHE.

RIGHT?
CHOMP

I SEE.
CHOMP

YEAH, SHE HAD A HUGE LUNCH.
CHOMP

CHOMP
CHOMP
CHOMP
CHOMP
SLURP
SLURP
SLURP

WHERE'S MY MEAL?
MEOW

MEOW MEOW
GRID
I'M HUNGWY.

GRIN GRIN
CHI, YOU'VE BEEN PRETTY FIRED UP TODAY.

AH, RIGHT!
I HEARD THAT BIG BLACK CAT WAS STIRRING UP TROUBLE AGAIN.

IT BROKE SOME FLOWER POTS.
IT EVEN RAN OFF WITH SOME SALMON.
SAL-MON?!
IT'S BACK?

WHAT KIND OF CAT DOES THAT?
THAT'S BOLD.

ONE WITH THIS FACE.
SQUEEZ

BLACK
AND ROLLY-POLLY.
TUG

MEOW
CHI HASN'T HAD ANYTHING TO EAT YET.

MEOW
THIS THING CAME BY...

AND A SLOW GAIT.
WITH SCARY EYES.

AND IT GULPED DOWN MY FOOD.
MEOW

MYA
AND GAWKED.
GAWK
IT GLARED
STARE
MYA

KINDA
HA HA

YOU KNOW?

I GUESS YOU HAD TO HAVE BEEN THERE.

HERE!
Forest Friends

AH!
RIGHT!

IT'S THIS KINDA CAT.
IT ALSO EATS SALMON.

OH!
WHA?

Brown Bear

Bear
A BEAR!
Kid's Almanac
Forest Friends
Kid's Almanac

THAT'S IT! ONE OF THOSE!
SHAA

WELL, NOT EXACTLY, BUT...
Forest Friends
SHAA

SHAA

NOW DO YOU SEE, DAD?

PAT

YUP, GOT IT.

PAT PAT

HOORAY! WE DID IT, YOHEI.

MEOW MEOW

YAY! WE DID IT!

STIK

STIK

YAMADA

Dear Residents,

We are experiencing a string of cat-related incidents.
If you happen to see the cat please contact me.

Super

the end

homemade 31: a cat uses her head

SIP SIP
STARE

WHAZ-ZAT?

IT'S MILK.
MILK

DO YOU WANT SOME?
HERE, TRY SOME COW'S MILK.
SPLISH

COW'S MILK.
COW MIULK?
LAP LAP LAP

HEY, I THOUGHT WE WEREN'T SUPPOSED TO GIVE HER REAL MILK.
WELL, A LITTLE WON'T HURT.
LAP LAP LAP
LIP LIP

COW MIULK...

SO TASTY !!
MEOW
GIMME MORE!

THONK
MILK
THANKS FOR THE SNACK.
THMP
THMP
THMP
!
COW MIULK!

MILK

COWWW
MIUUULK

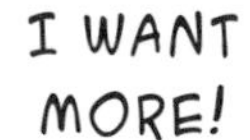
I WANT
MORE!

BUT HOW DO I GET IT?

WHICH ONE, YOHEI?
THIS ONE.
CORN CEREAL

I'LL ASK MOMMY!

MIYA
MOMMY, GET ME SOME COW MIULK.
SAUNTER
SAUNTER
SAUNTER

MEW
MIULK PWEASE.
OKAY
SHAK
SHAK
CORN CEREAL

MIULK
MEOW
SHMP
SHMP
SHMP
MILK
WHOOSH
COW MIULK !!
HEY!
WHERE'S MY MIULK ?
SHMP
SHMP
SHMP
WHERE'S YOUR BOWL?
HERE !
CORN CEREAL
MILK

CORN CEREAL
ZAK
ZAK

NOW
MILK
SOME MILK.

SPLOO
SPLOO
SPLOO

SPLOOSH
SPLOOSH
NOW I SEE!

DASH

MEOW
POUR SOME FOR CHI NOW.

HERE'S MY DISH.
IT'S GOT CRUNCHIES, TOO.
TINK
TINK
MIYAN

MEOW
TINK
TINK
TINK
MILK
CORN CEREAL
TINK
TINK

ALL RIGHT.
I'LL GIVE CHI SOME, TOO.

SLURP

COW MIULK!

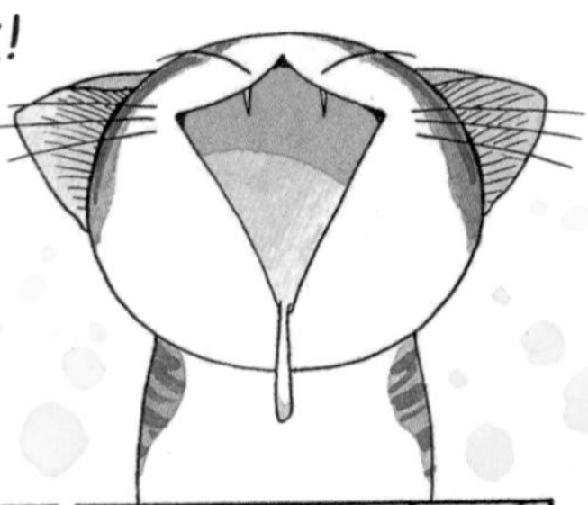

LOOK, MORE OF YOUR FAVORITE.
SO CRUNCHY!

ZAK ZAK
CAT FOOD DRY

ZAK
ZAK
ZAK

HUH ?

THAT'S NOT WHAT I MEANT.
MILK

COW
MIULK!

HOW DO I GET SOME?

GOT IT!

SHUV
SHUV

SKOOT
SKOOT

MY!
HOW NIMBLE!
MILK

MEOW
MI

GIMME
SOME
OF THAT
MIULK.

MILK
SHOOMP

COW MIULK

WANNA JOIN US, CHI?

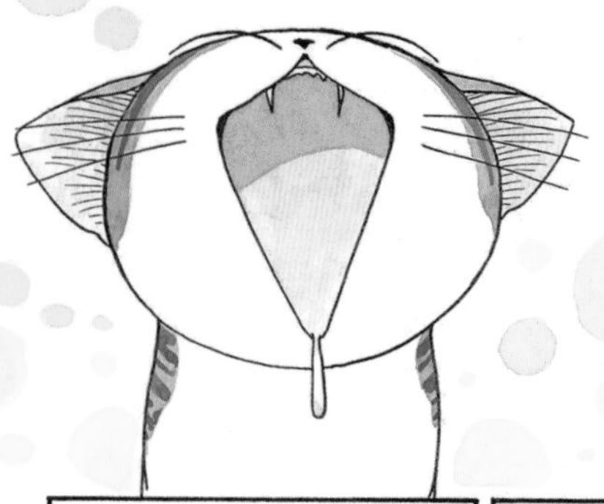

YOU DROPPED SOME.
THERE

POP

HEY?!

SHMP
SHMP
SHMP

SHOOM
ARGH!
THUNK
MILK
POW
GLOOM

I'M HOME.
WHUMP
MARKET
MILK

COW...
COW...
COW...
COW...
MILK
MARKET

COW MIULK!

KRSH KRSH KRSH
MIULK! COW MIULK!

ZING

MYA
MOMMY, DEFINITELY MIULK, OKAY?
MILK

YOU WANT IT, CHI?

SHIVER

COW MIULK

YOU LOVE PLASTIC BAGS, DON'T YOU?

BOBBL

MILK

WHAM
I DON'T WANT THIS! I WANT THAT MIULK!
MEOW
RUSTL RUSTL RUSTL

COWWW MIUUULK
RUSTL RUSTL

COW MIULK
RUSTL RUSTL

MIU-LK
RUSTL RUSTL RUSTL

RUSTL RUSTL RUSTL RUSTL

RUSTL RUSTL RUSTL RUSTL RUSTL RUSTL RUSTL RUSTL RUSTL RUSTL RUSTL

MIYA

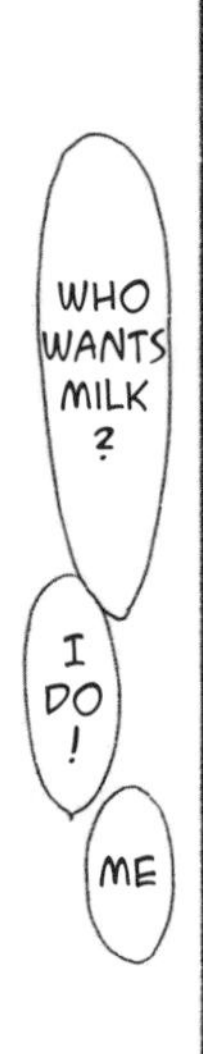
WHO WANTS MILK?
I DO!
ME

WANT SOME, CHI?
MILK
MEOW
GUESS SHE'S TOO BUSY TO HEAR YOU!
RUSTL RUSTL RUSTL

the end

homemade 32: a cat aggravates

KOFF
KOFF
HUFF
HUFF
SKAMPER

KOFF
KOFF
PHOO

JUST STAY IN BED TODAY, OKAY?
KOFF
KOFF
HUFF

YEAH
I'LL SLEEP.

WE'LL BE BACK.
SLAM

TAP TAP TAP TAP
MIYA
WHAT ARE YOU DOING, DADDY?
CHI.
ARE YOU WORRIED ABOUT ME?
HOW SWEET.
MEOW?
WHAT'S ON YA HEAD, DADDY?
GRAB
UH?
GRIP GRIP GRIP
HEY!
STOP THAT.
SKKKEE

MIYA
IT CAME OFF.
CHI.

KOFF
HEY, GIVE THAT BACK.
MEW
WHAT THE?
SMAK
SMAK

SQUEEZ

LET'S PLAY !

TUG OF WAR!!
MEOW MEOW
HUFF HUFF
CHI.
I'VE GOT A FEVER.
YANK YANK

YOINK

HUFF
STICK

HAH

DADDY WON.

WATER?

I'LL TAKE A SIP.
MIYA

HEY!

SQUEEEZE

HUH ?
KLANK
KLANK
KLANK

AH!
GASP
KLANK
KLANK
KLANK
KLANK
HEEE
MEOOW
WET!
...
HUFF
HUFF
KOFF
KOFF
ARGH
SWIFF
SWIFF
SWIFF
LIK
LIK
LIK
HUFF
HUFF
CHI

STAY OUT OF THIS ROOM, 'KAY.
HUFF HUFF
HUFF HUFF
SHOOMP
SMAK
WHAT'S WRONG, DADDY?
MEW
SKFF SKFF SKFF SKFF SKFF SKFF SKFF
MEW MEW
MEW MEW
HEY, DADDY.
OH?!
HUSH

MEOW
I SAW SOME PREY!
SKFF
SKFF
SKFF
MEOW
I SAW IT! I SAW IT!
MEOW
DADDY! DAD-DY!
MEOW
DASH

KABLAM

HUSH

PHEW, ALL RIGHT!
DROWZ

SKTTTT
SKTTTT
SKTTTT
SKTTTT
JUST HOLD ON...
SHE CAN'T COME IN.

MIYA?
WHAZ-ZUP, DADDY?
HEH

...

MEOW
LET'S PLAY!
BOOF
BOOF
BOOF
BOOF
BOOF

...
DART
MYA
MYA
MYA

WE'RE HOME.
DID YOU REST MUCH?
HUFF
HUFF
WELL, I GOT HER TO SLEEP...
HUFF HUFF
HUFF
WRECKED

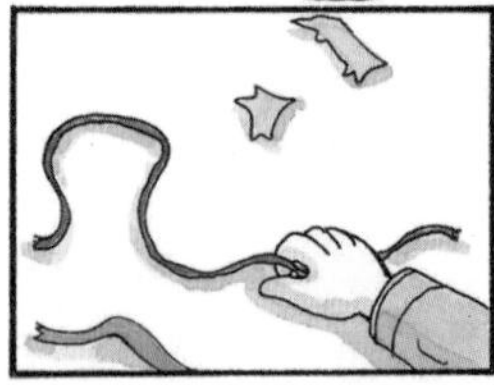

ZZZ

the end

homemade 33: a cat searches

FLOP

THIS SPOT IS A LITTLE HARD.

VOOM

SHIFF SHIFF
SHIFF
MYAAH
NAP-TIME, YOHEY.

IT'S MUSHIER HERE.

HUH ?

VOOM

VOOM! SHOOM!
HANG

VOOM
YOHEY JUST MOVES AROUND TOO MUCH.

...

MOOSH
MOOSH
FLUFF
MIYA
NAP-TIME, MOMMY.
SHFF
SHFF
SHFF
SO FWUFFY!
WHUMF
MEOW

GO PLAY OVER THERE.
YOINK

THERE MUST BE A GOOD PLACE.

WANDER WANDER

WELL, I GUESS.
SHFF SHFF

NAP-TIME, DADDY.
MIYA

BUDUM
BUDUM

HEY?

BUDUM
BUDUM
I
WONDER.
BUDUM
BUDUM

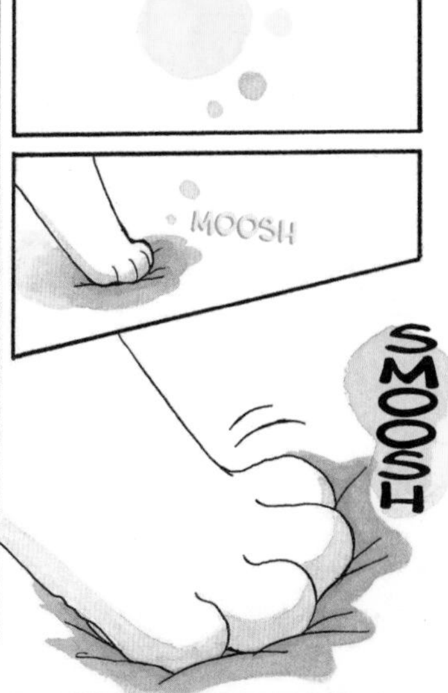

HUH?

SMUSH
MOOSH
SMUSH
MOOSH

HEY, WHAT ARE YOU LOOKING FOR, ALL SERIOUS?
SMUSH
MOOSH
SMUSH
MOOSH

SMUSH
MOOSH

SMUSH

SMUSH

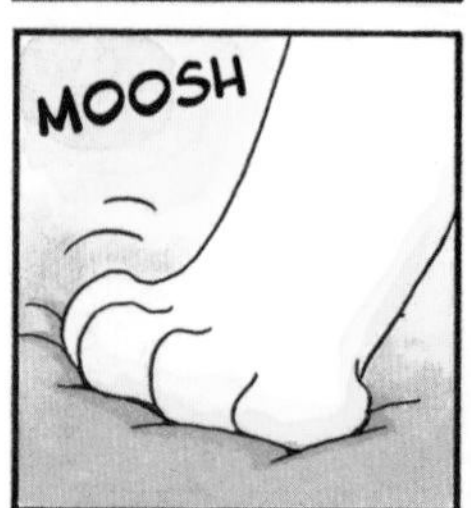
MOOSH

AHHH!

NUZZLE

SNUGGL
SNUGGL

NUZZL

AH, CHI.

NUZZL

SHE JUST DUG IN,
BURIED HER HEAD AND CONKED OUT.

MAKES ME THINKS THAT SHE REALLY LIKES ME, HEH.
HA HA HA

SNUGGL

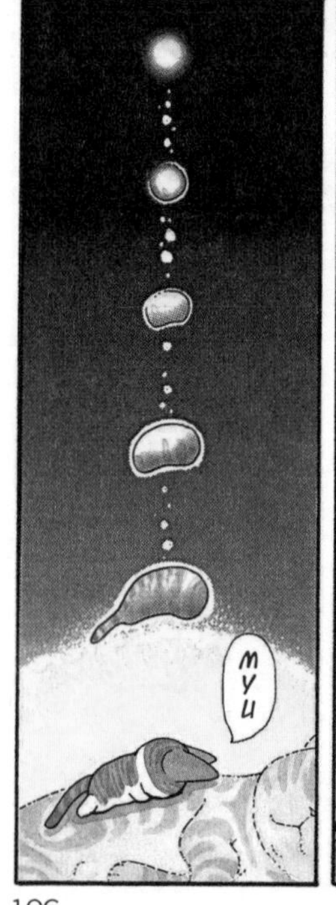
MYU

I WONDER WHAT THIS FEELWING IS?

the end

homemade 34: a cat stalks

SLINK
SLINK
WHAT'S IT HERE FOR TODAY?

RUSTL
RUSTL

SHAK

USING CHI'S YARD AS A PATHWAY?

HEY, SO WHERE CAN YOU SNEAK THROUGH FROM HERE?
MYA?

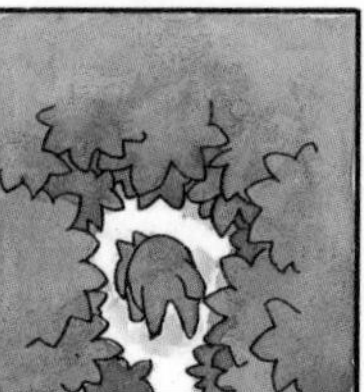

WHAT'S IT DOING?

SHAK

SKUTTL

MUNCH
MUNCH
MUNCH

WHATCHA DOING?
MIYA?

MEOW?
MUNCH
MUNCH
MUNCH
MUNCH
YO.
NYAN

TASTY?
MEW?

MUNCH
MUNCH
NYA
WELL, IN MODERATION IT'S GOOD FOR OUR SPECIES.

OUR SHPE-CIES?
MYA?

NN
OUR KIND, THAT IS.
SMAK

OUR KIND?

MEYOW
MEOW
YOU'RE WRONG.
CHI'S KIND ARE YOHEY, DADDY AND MOMMY.
...
KOH KOH KOH
BLECH
RUSTL
MEOW
RIGHT? RIGHT?
SKUTTL
LATER.
NYA
MEOW
WAS IT YUCKY?
OH?

MIYA
I FOUND YA!

MEOW
HIDE-N-SEEK!

BLAM
BAH

MEOW
WHAT'S GOWING ON?

GLARE

?!

SNFF
SNFF
SNFF

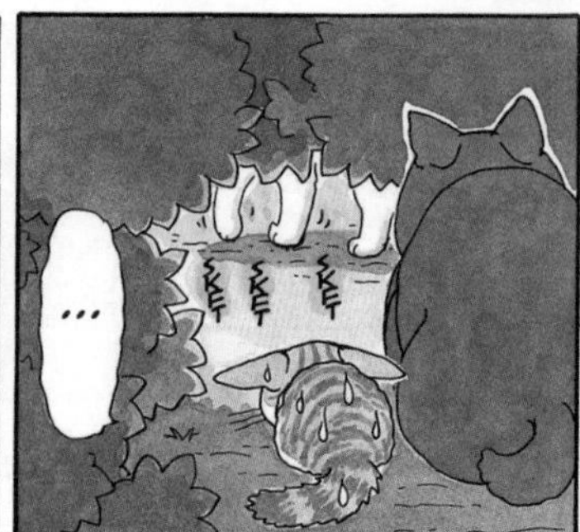
...
SKET SKET SKET

OH, I DON'T LIKE THOSE.

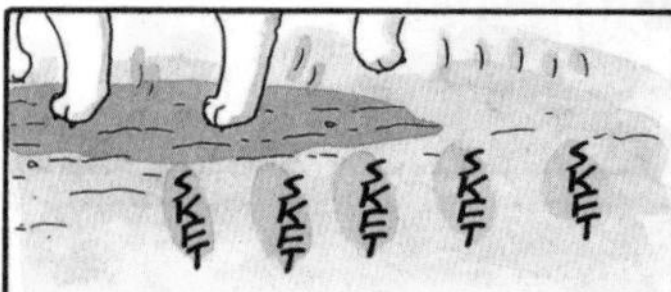
SKET SKET SKET SKET SKET

PANT
PANT
SKET
SKET
SKET

AHH

THAT WAS SOME SCAREWY HIDE-N-SEEK.

SLINK SLINK

I HAVE TO GET BETTER AT HIDE-N-SEEK.
MEOW
DROOFS

NYAN
YOU NEED NOT FEAR THEM IF YOU'RE ABOVE THEM.

MIYA
REALLY?

BUT CHI CAN'T CLIMB UP THERE.
MIYAN
BOING
BOING
BOING

NYAA
IT'S ALL RIGHT.

YOU WILL IN TIME.

REALLY ?!
MYA!
OF COURSE. YOU ARE A CAT, AFTER ALL.
NIYA
NYA
LATER.

K...AT?

MEOW
NO WAY.
I'M NOT A CAT.
I'M CHI!
MEOW

the end

homemade 35: a cat goes home

GOWING HOME.

TIP TIP TIP

WAIT?

WHICH WAY IS HOME?
AND WHERE AM I?

...

TWEET

HEY?!

I THINK I'VE BEEN HERE BEFORE.

WHEN?
WHEN WAS IT?

...?

BOW WOW
BOW
BOW
BARK
ZING

ONE OF THOSE GUYS IS COMING! WHAT NOW?

!
RIGHT, I'LL HIDE-N-SEEK!

RUSTLE

BOW WOW
HUFF
HUFF

BARK

BOW WOW
HUFF
HUFF
TITTER TITTER

BARK
HUFF
HUFF
TITTER TITTER

TITTER TITTER

MIYA!
CHI DID IT!

TILT

WHICH WAY IS HOME?
!

I'M SURE IT'S THAT WAY.

I'M GOWING HOME.
SKAMPER

THIS WAY.
SKAMPER

SKAMPER
AND THIS WAY.

OH!

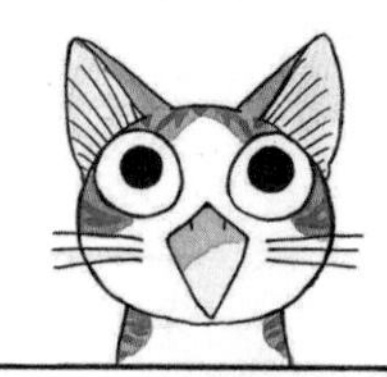

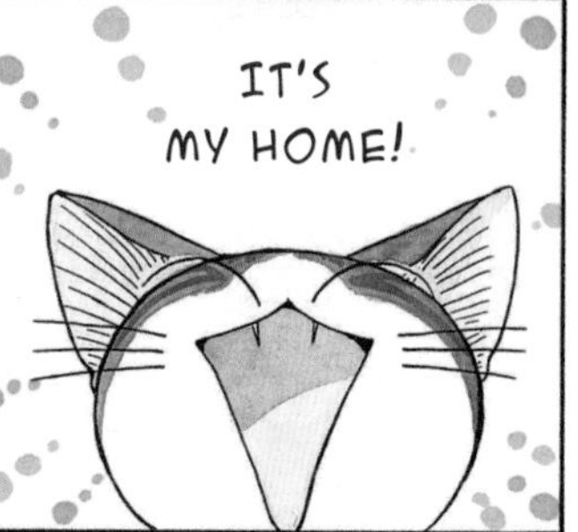

IT'S MY HOME!

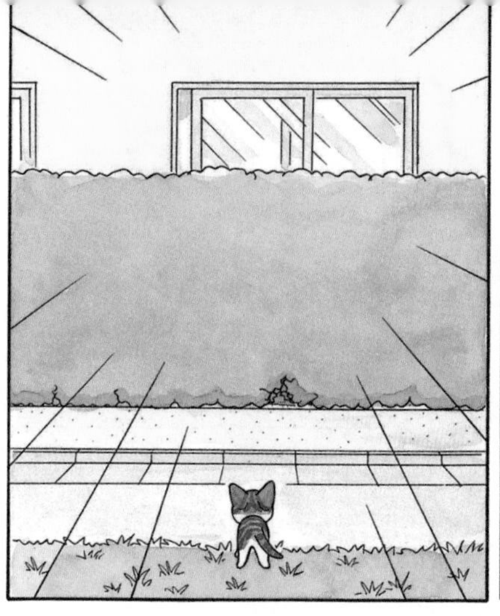

YAY, I'M HOME!

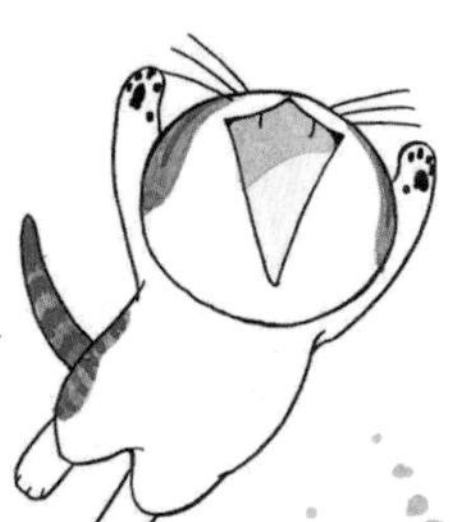

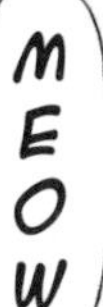

MEOW

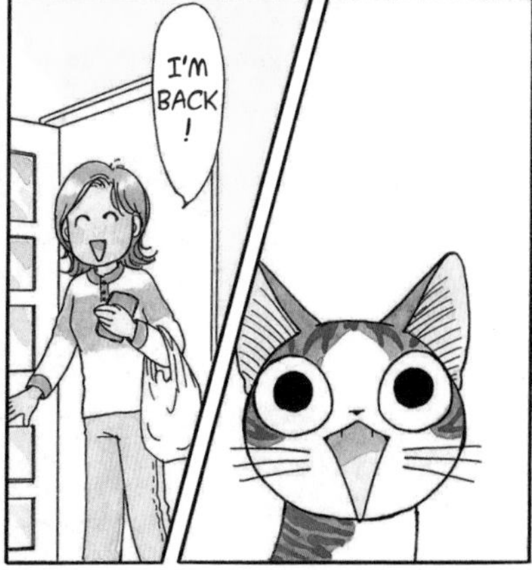

I'M BACK!

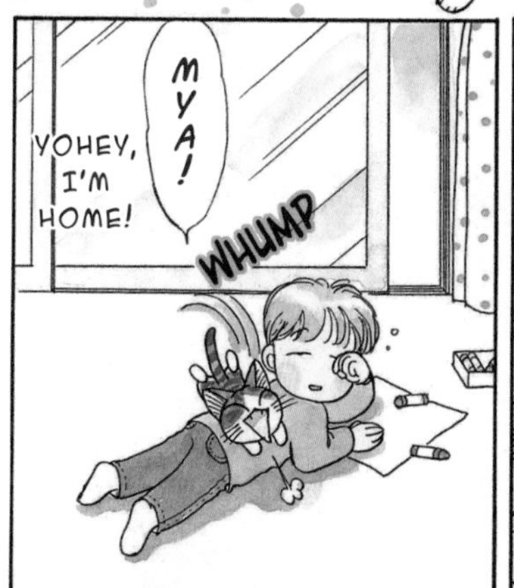

MYA!
YOHEY, I'M HOME!
WHUMP

MEOW!
MOMMY, I'M HOME!

I'M HOME!

MEOW!
DADDY, I'M HOME!

MIYAN
EVEWYONE, I'M HOME!

DID SOMETHING GOOD HAPPEN?
IN A GOOD MOOD, CHI?

...?

the end

homemade 36: a cat resists

CHI NEEDS TO GET HER VACCINES, SO WE'RE GOING TO THE VET'S AGAIN.

PRE-EMPTIVE SAFETY CHECK.
VIP
VIP
AH!
CHI, WAIT!
NOT THAT!
SKAT
IT'S NOT SAFE TO GO OUT NOW.
CHI!
DASH
HONEY!
!

SKAMPER

DART

UH-OH...

CHI'S ESCAPED!

WAAAH

KYAA

HURRY!

AND THE SUPER'S OUT THERE!

SKAT

STICK

PANT

PANT

HAH

CHI'S NOT GOWING.

UHHHHH!

WHAT NOW?
SHOOP
AH,
IF I HURRY I MIGHT BE ABLE TO CATCH HER.

GOOD LUCK, DEAR.
RIGHT!

SNORT
ZOOM

SHOO

!
OH, MR. YAMADA.
BAM

MY, YOU'RE IN A HURRY.

DRAT ...

WELL, UM, NOT REALLY.
YOU SEE.
THERE'S ...

WOAH

WELL, I JUST FELT HIGH FROM
HOW GREAT THE GREENERY LOOKS.
HA HA HA HA
THEY ARE NICE.

WELL THEN
TURN

AH!
SWIPE
SWIPE SWIPE

WHAT IS THE MAT-TER?
SWIPE SWIPE
BUMBL
OH
WE SURE ARE HAVING NICE WEATHER TODAY.
QUITE
BYE
TURN
ARGH!
BUMBL
WHAT NOW?
SPIN
OH, UMM...
WELL
YOU SEE...
HMM?

TURN
BYE, THEN.
Dear Residents,
We are experiencing a string of cat-related incidents.
u happen to see the
please contact me.
Super
GAPE GAPE
Dear Residents,
We are experiencing string of cat-related incidents.
you happen to see the cat please contact me.
I GIVE UP!
OH!
EH !!
TURN
SHUMP

AH! THAT CAT!
DART
WAIT, YOU!
DASH
WAIT!

THAT BLACK THING'S AMAZING! HE HUNTS?

HEY?

OF ALL THINGS, THE BEAR CAT SAVED THE DAY.
THAT WAS CLOSE.
GOTCHA!

AND WHAT WAS CHI DOING AGAIN?

the end

homemade 37: a cat is defiant

TODAY WE ARE DEFINITELY GOING TO SEE THE VET.
I DON'T WANNA.
MEOW
FLAP
FLAP

STOP THAT, DADDY!
MEOWR
NUDGE NUDGE

I THINK SHE KNOWS FROM THE BASKET THAT YOU'RE TAKING HER TO THE VET.

COME HERE, CHI.
YEAH
HIDE IT HERE.
THINK THIS THROUGH, A BIT.
FLUT
NO WAY!
CHI
FWIP
FWIP
FWIP
HMM?
THE CAGE IS GONE.
FWIP
FWIP
FWIP
FWIP
WOWWW
MYAA
CHI WANTS TO PLAY, TOO!
DART

MIYA
WHAP
NOW!
SUC-CESS!
MEOW!
MOMMY TRICKED ME!
NO!
MYA!

GOTTA RUN!
GOTTA RUN!
TATAKS
MEOW
SKAMPER
YEOUCH!
GOTTA HIDE!
FUMBL FUMBL
CHI
THERE YOU ARE.

POKE
POKE

LEER

MIYA
I FOUND A GOOD PWACE, HUH?

MIYA
IN HERE THERE'S NO WAY MOMMY OR DADDY CAN CATCH ME.

GOTCHA!
ZIP

HUH?
MEW

YOHEY?!

NICE JOB, YOHEI.
YOU NETTED A LIVE ONE.
KLAP KLAP

FWUMP

WHAT DO YA THINK YOU'RE DOING?!
MEOWR
SHUV
SHUV

YOHEY!
MIYA
SHUV
SHUV

SEE YOU SOON, CHI.
!

GRIN
GRIN
GRIN
GRIN

...

FUMP

TWAITOR!

BOBBL
BOBBL
BOBBL
MEOW
MEOWN
BOBBL
BOBBL

MEOWWWR
I THOUGHT YOU WERE MY BUDDIES!

the end

homemade 38: a cat sulks

GWAH
FSSSK
GAK

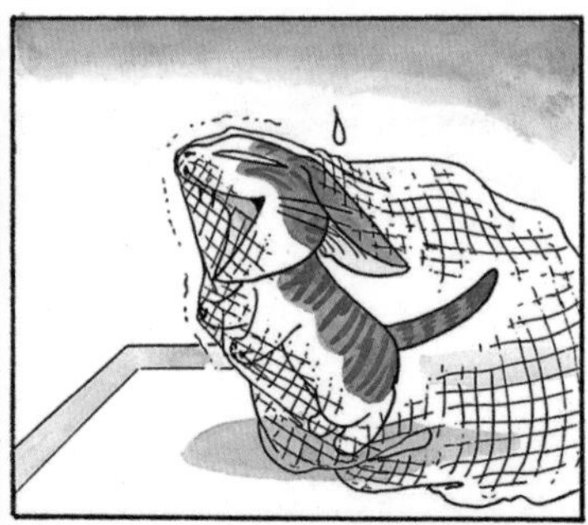

PINCH

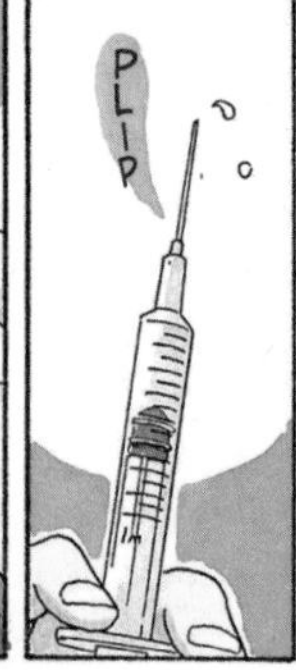
PLIP

?!

MREOW
WHAT'S GOWING ON!

HEY, WHAT ARE YOU UP TO?

NYAN

MEOW
CHI'S RUN AWAY.
SKAT

EVEWYONE'S BEEN PICKING ON ME.
MIYAHN

I THOUGHT THEY WERE MY BUDDIES.
MIYAAN

FWIP

SKF
SKF
SKF
UNG
I SEE.

HUH?
WELL, THAT'S HOW IT IS.
NYAN
SKF
SKF
SKF
SKF
WAIT, WHAT IS?
MEW?

HRM
JUST DON'T TRUST HUMANS TOO MUCH.
UNN

ZAPT
RIGHT! YOU CAN'T TWUST THEM!
MIYA

AND WHAT DOES "TWUST" MEAN?
MIU
TO THINK THEY'RE YOUR KIND.
NYAN
CUZ THEY AREN'T YOUR KIND.

MYA
THAT'S RIGHT, THEY AREN'T MY KIND.
MIYA
RIGHT?
NYAN
CORRECT.
MIYA
RIGHT?
NYAN
CORRECT.
ZASH
SHOOP
NYA
LATER
MYA
BYE
HEY, WHERE YA GOWING?
MYA

NYAN
I'M GOING HOME TO EAT.

?

NYAN
EVERY-ONE'S WAITING.

HUH?!

NYAN
I SCRATCH THEIR BACKS, THEY SCRATCH MINE...

WHAT?!

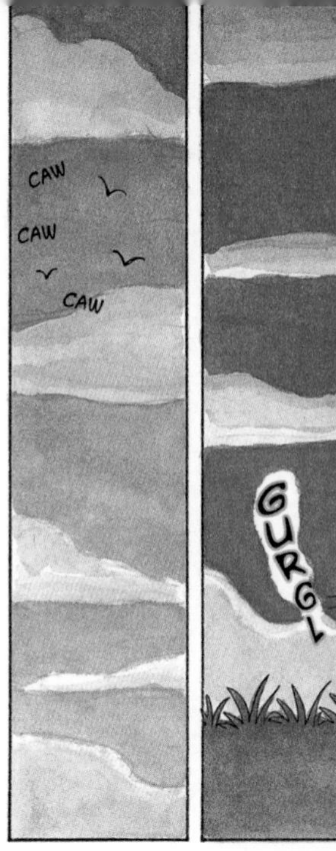
CAW
CAW
CAW

...
GURGL

SNEAK
IT'S CHI!
CHI'S BACK!
PHEW! WHERE'D YOU GO? WE WERE WORRIED.

HEH, I'M ONLY BACK FOR DINNER...

LET'S EAT!
YAY, HAND-ROLLED SUSHI!
LOOKS GOOD.
WANNA TRY SOME, CHI?
SKOOT
COME JOIN US, CHI.

BLOX
WHAZ-ZAT?
BLOX
WHUMP
CHI, IT'S TUNA.
I'VE GOT EGG.
SALMON EGGS FOR ME.
TUNA FIRST FOR ME.
MEOW
IS THIS CHI'S?

PIK
PIK

LIK
LIK

MUNCH
MUNCH

HUMMINA

SO T-TASTY!

CHI

ISN'T IT GOOD?
TASTY HUH, CHI.
WAS YOUR'S GOOD, CHI?

CHI
HUMMINA
HUMMINA

FLUTTER

TASTY, YEAH?
MYA

I'M GLAD YOU LIKED IT.
PAT PAT PAT

PURR
PURR

GRIN

SAY, LET'S STAY BUDDIES AFTER ALL!
MIYA

the end

special menu a cat meets FukuFuku

UNYA?

MYA
FLUT
FLUT
WAIT UP!

WHAP

FLUT
FLUT

MEOW
YOOHOOOO
IT'S FWYING!

...

MYA
KYAA
YEAHHH

FWIP
SHFT
SHFT

MYA
AH

MEOW
WHEE

MEOW
WOAH

MIYA
FLUTTER
WAIT, OVER HERE!

MEOW
THIS IS FUN.
FLUTTER

FLUTTER

FLUTTER

SNAP

GLARE

UGYA

PIK PIK

WHAT IZZIT ?
MIYA
SWIPE SWIPE SWIPE

GASP

FLUT

FLUT
FLUT

FLUT

FLUT

FROU

FROU

FLUT

BLINK BLINK
NUZZL
MYAH
SAY, ISN'T THIS FUN?
MEOW MEOW
...
SWIPE SWIPE SWIPE

the end

A Note on the Special Chapter

Ms. Kanata's comic career spans over three decades, with the vast majority of her works focusing on the lives of household pets. Her debut work *Petit Cat Jam-Jam*, a *shojo* (girls') comic, distinguished her as one of the best graphic storytellers for young audiences, but it was her first hit *FukuFuku Funyan* with which Ms. Kanata's cats took Japan, and eventually the world, by storm.

Premiering in women's anthology *Me* in 1988, *FukuFuku Funyan* took pet comics to new levels of recognition. While the series ran, *Me*'s editorial staff was flooded with letters from readers of all ages detailing their personal feline experiences. Cat lovers saw just how well Ms. Kanata understood and rendered feline behavior.

In 2004, *Chi's Sweet Home* started running in Kodansha's comics anthology *Morning*. Though writing for a flagship *seinen* (men's) weekly marked a bit of a departure for Ms. Kanata, it was a highly successful one. Her first feline star FukuFuku makes an appearance in the special chapter exclusive to the graphic novel edition, giving new fans of Ms. Kanata a chance to become acquainted with this other kitty idol.

A relatively plump calico, FukuFuku is notorious for her poor eyesight, grumpiness, and tendency for napping too much. Though her interactions with Chi are characteristic of her behavior in her own series, they only reveal a small glimpse into her history and personality. While it's FukuFuku's only appearance in *Chi's Sweet Home* to date, in the coming volumes readers can look forward to a wide range of furry and feathery friends to follow and support.

PREVIEW
LICK LICK
LICK
NEIGH
BOW WOW

© Kou Yaginuma

Chi's Sweet Home, volume 2

Translation - Ed Chavez
Production - Hiroko Mizuno
Glen Isip

First published in Japan in 2005 by Kodansha, Ltd., Tokyo
Publication for this English edition arranged through Kodansha, Ltd., Tokyo
English language version produced by Vertical, Inc.

Translation provided by Vertical, Inc., 2010
Published by Vertical, Inc., New York

Originally published in Japanese as *Chiizu Suiito Houmu* by Kodansha, Ltd., 2005
Chiizu Suiito Houmu first serialized in *Morning*, Kodansha, Ltd., 2004-

This is a work of fiction.

ISBN: 978-1-934287-85-9

Manufactured in China

First Edition

Second Printing

Vertical, Inc.
451 Park Avenue South, 7th Floor
New York, NY 10016
www.vertical-inc.com

Special thanks to K. Kitamoto